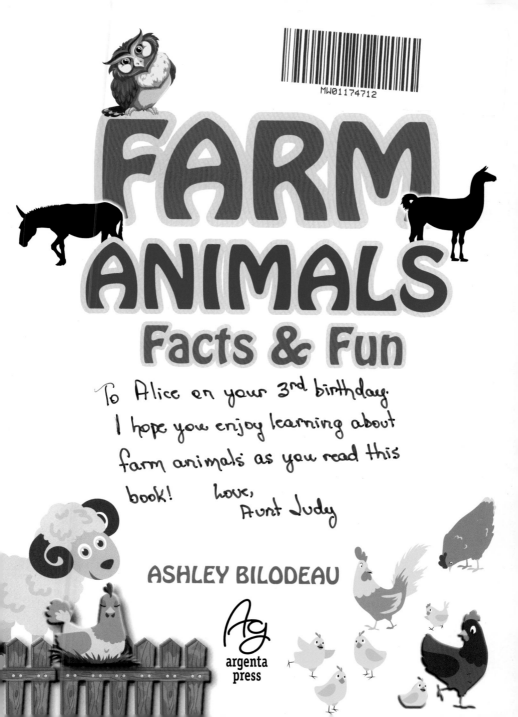

FARM ANIMALS
Facts & Fun

*To Alice en your 3rd birthday.
I hope you enjoy learning about
farm animals as you read this
book!   love,
          Aunt Judy*

ASHLEY BILODEAU

argenta
press

Contents

Introduction 4

Places at the Farm 6

Horses 10

Cattle 14

Goats 18

Sheep 22

Donkeys 26

Pigs 28

Rabbits 32

Chickens 36

Roosters 40

Turkeys 42

Geese 44

Ducks 46

Dogs 48

Cats 50

Barn Owls 52

Elk, Bison and Deer 54

Alpacas and Llamas 58

Honeybees 60

Fish 62

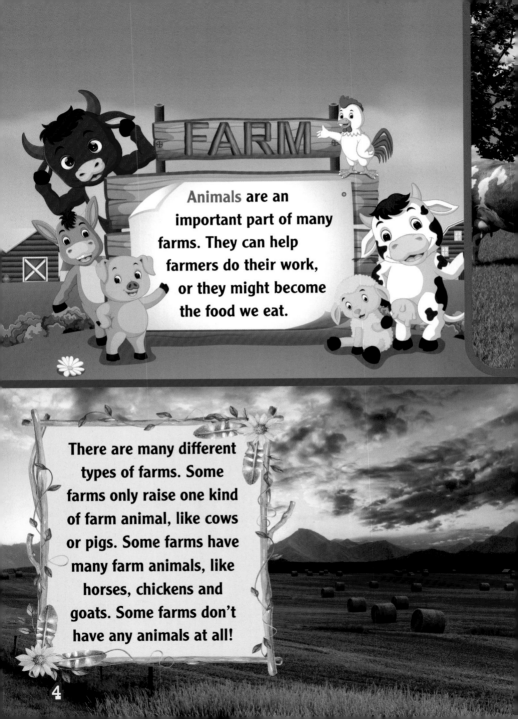

Animals are an important part of many farms. They can help farmers do their work, or they might become the food we eat.

There are many different types of farms. Some farms only raise one kind of farm animal, like cows or pigs. Some farms have many farm animals, like horses, chickens and goats. Some farms don't have any animals at all!

Places at the Farm

The pasture is a big, open field with grasses and other plants.
If you visit a farm, you might see horses, cows, sheep, goats and pigs roaming the pasture and grazing.

The **barn** is a big building where farmers store feed for the animals, hay, tools or even vehicles. Some animals might also sleep in the barn! The barn can protect the animals from wind, rain or snow while they're sleeping.

The coop is a shelter for the chickens. Because the coop is for chickens, it is called a chicken coop! Chickens lay eggs, rest and sleep inside the coop.

The **pen** is a fenced space outside. The fence keeps the animals in one place. Sheep, cows, horses and pigs can all be kept inside a pen.

Horses

Horses are great helpers! They can pull heavy wagons and farm machines to do things like spreading soil or feed for the other animals.

Horses are herbivores. That means they only eat plants like grass and some weeds.

Farmers often ride horses to help herd the other farm animals. People also ride horses for fun!

11

A male horse is called a stallion, and a female horse is called a mare. A baby horse is called a foal.

Did you know?

- Horses sleep standing up!
- Horses can't breathe through their mouth! They can only breathe through their nose.

What did the horse say when it fell?

I can't giddyup!

Cattle

You can find two different types of cattle on a farm. Dairy cattle produce the milk that we drink, and beef cattle give us meat like steak, roasts and hamburgers!

15

Goats

Goats are raised for milk, meat and fiber for clothing.

What do goats like to eat for breakfast?

Goatmeal!

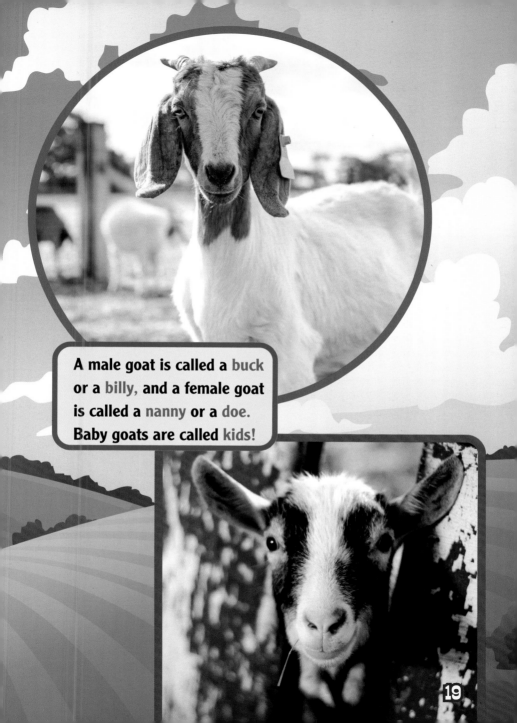

A male goat is called a buck or a billy, and a female goat is called a nanny or a doe. Baby goats are called kids!

Goats are great friends. They love to spend time with their herd, other animals and people.

20

Did you know?

- Goat milk is the most popular type of milk in the world!

- Goats have rectangular pupils. This helps them to see almost everything around them—except for what is right behind them.

Sheep

Sheep are raised for milk, meat and wool.

A group of sheep is called a flock.

A male sheep is called a ram, and a female sheep is called a ewe. Baby sheep are called lambs.

A sheep's wool is removed once every year. This is called shearing. Their wool is turned into yarn that can be used to make clothes, hats, blankets and more!

What do you call a sheep who likes to dance?

A baaa-llerina!

Did you know?

- Just like goats, sheep have rectangular pupils.
- A sheep's wool never stops growing!
- There are more than 1000 breeds of sheep around the world.

Donkeys

Donkeys are great guard animals. They protect the other farm animals from coyotes and other predators. A predator is an animal that hunts other animals to eat.

Donkeys are also very strong. They can carry heavy loads or pull a cart or a plow.

A male donkey is called a jack, and a female donkey is called a jennet or a jenny. A baby donkey is called a foal.

Did you know?

- Donkeys can live for more than 50 years!
- Donkeys love bananas! They even eat the peel!

27

Pigs

Pigs are raised for meat.

A male pig is called a boar, and a female pig is called a sow. Baby pigs are called piglets.

Pigs will eat almost anything! Broken eggs, sour milk, table scraps… you name it!

Did you know?

- Pigs can't sweat! They like to roll around in the mud to keep cool.
- Pigs can dream!

31

Rabbits

Rabbits are raised for meat, fertilizer, wool and pelts.

A male rabbit is called a buck, and a female rabbit is called a doe. Baby rabbits are called bunnies.

A group of bunnies is called a colony or a nest.

A rabbit pen is called a hutch.

Hip-hop!

What is a rabbit's favorite type of dance?

34

Did you know?

- A rabbit's teeth never stop growing! They keep their teeth short by chewing on grass, wildflowers and vegetables.
- Rabbits purr when they are happy!

Chickens

Chickens are raised for meat and for their eggs.

A female chicken is called a hen. Baby chickens are called chicks!

A group of chickens is called a flock.

37

Did you know?

- Chickens are related to the Tyrannosaurus rex!
- You can tell if a chicken will lay a white or brown egg by the color of their earlobes! Chickens with white earlobes lay white eggs, and chickens with red earlobes lay brown eggs.

Roosters

Why did the rooster cross the road? To cock-a-doodle-doo something!

A rooster is a male chicken.

When a male chicken is less than one year old, it is called a cockerel.

Roosters protect the hens from predators and break up hen fights.

Did you know?

• You have probably heard that roosters crow at sunrise, and that's true! But roosters also like to crow at all times during the day.

41

Turkeys

Turkeys are raised for meat.

Male turkeys are called gobblers, and female turkeys are called hens. A baby turkey is called a poult.

Only male turkeys gobble, but all turkeys make other sounds, like purrs, yelps and kee-kees.

What side of the turkey has the most feathers? The outside!

Did you know?

- A turkey's head can change color when it feels calm or excited! The color can change from red to blue to white.

- You can tell if a turkey is male or female by the shape of its poop! A male turkey's poop looks like a "J," and a female turkey's poop looks like a spiral.

Geese

Geese are raised for their eggs, meat and feathers.

Geese help protect hens from predators. Geese can also be good for the garden! They eat weeds, worms, slugs and other pests that can harm the crops.

A male goose is called a gander, and a female goose is called a goose. A baby goose is called a gosling.

Did you know?

- A group of geese is called a skein when they fly and a gaggle when they're on the ground.
- Geese can live up to 25 years!

What happened to the goose when it fell down the hill?

It got goose bumps!

Ducks

Ducks are raised for meat and for their eggs.

A male duck is called a drake, and a female duck is called a hen. A baby duck is called a duckling.

Ducks are omnivores. That means they eat plants and bugs. Ducks can help protect the garden by eating the bugs that can harm the fruits and vegetables.

Did you know?

- A duck's feathers are waterproof! Even when they dive underwater, their skin stays dry.
- A duck egg is larger than a chicken egg and has a harder shell.

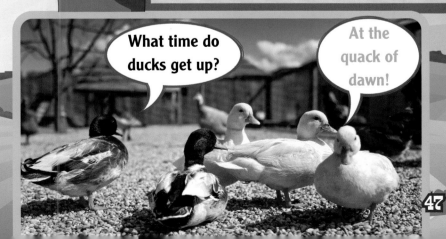

What time do ducks get up?

At the quack of dawn!

Dogs

Farm dogs love to have jobs, too!

Guardian dogs protect farm animals from wolves, coyotes and other predators.

Herding dogs gather livestock, like cattle and sheep, to keep them from wandering off.

Did you know?

- Dogs can only sweat through the pads on their feet!
- They also pant to keep cool.

What farm animal keeps the best time?

A watch dog!

49

Cats

Farm cats are often called barn cats.

Barn cats spend their time eating bugs and hunting mice, rats and other rodents and pests.

Did you know?

- Cats have 18 toes!
  Each front paw has
  5 toes, and each
  back paw has 4 toes.

Barn Owls

Barn owls can be useful on a farm. They hunt mice and other rodents.

Barn owls get their name because they are known to nest in barns. They will also nest in other buildings and structures, like grain silos or sheds.

Did you know?

- A barn owl's wingspan is almost one meter (3 feet) long!

- Barn owls are about the size of a cat, but only weigh one pound (454 grams)! That is the same weight as a block of butter.

- Because barn owls are so light and their wingspan is so long, they are able to fly slowly, which makes it easier to hunt for prey.

Knock, knock.

Who's there?

Owl.

Owl, who?

Owl be seeing you!

Elk, Bison and Deer

Bison, elk and deer are raised for their meat.

Elk meat and deer meat are called venison.

Some elk are raised for the velvet from their antlers. The velvet is used in some medicines.

A baby deer is called a fawn.
A baby bison is called a red dog.
A baby elk is called a calf.

Did you know?

- A group of elk is called a gang.
- Bison are the largest land mammal in North America.
- A deer's eyes are on the side of its head, so they can see more of what is around them.

Who puts money under the deer's pillow?

The hoof fairy!

Alpacas and Llamas

Alpacas are raised for their fleece. It is spun into yarn.

Alpaca

Llama

A llama can be raised for its wool, but they make great guard animals, too! They protect the other animals from predators, like wolves and foxes.

Alpaca

A male alpaca is called a sire, and a female alpaca is called a dam. A female alpaca that has not given birth is called a maiden.

A male llama is called a macho, and a female llama is called a hembra.

What is a llama's favorite drink?

Llamanade!

Did you know?

- Alpacas and llamas are part of an animal group called camelids.
- Camelids will spit or stick out their tongue when they are annoyed.

Honeybees

Honeybees **are raised** to make honey.

A honeybee farm is called an **apiary**.

The honeybees are kept in beehives where they make honeycombs. The beekeeper pulls the honeycombs out of the beehive to collect the honey.

Did you know?

- Honeybees don't sleep! Instead, they rest by holding perfectly still.
- A beehive can have up to 100,000 bees inside!
- Honeybees dance when they find nectar or pollen! Their dance tells the other bees where to go.

What do bees chew?

Bumblegum!

Fish

Fish farms raise fish for food.

Some fish farms raise the fish in tanks. Other fish farms raise the fish in an enclosed area of an ocean, lake or river.

Did you know?

- The most popular fish raised in fish farms are carp and tilapia.

Where does a fish keep its money?

The riverbank!

The Publisher: Argenta Press is an imprint of Dragon Hill Publishing Ltd.
Library and Archives Canada Cataloguing in Publication
Title: Farm animals : facts & funny / Ashley Bilodeau.
Names: Bilodeau, Ashley, 1995- author.
Identifiers: Canadiana (print) 2022014205X | Canadiana (ebook) 20220142114 | ISBN 9781988294049 (softcover) | ISBN 9781988294056 (PDF)
Subjects: LCSH: Domestic animals—Juvenile literature.
Classification: LCC SF75.5 .B55 2022 | DDC j636—dc23

Project Manager: Marina Michaelides
Layout & Design: Ryschell Dragunov

Front cover: GettyImages: by-studio; Halyna Dorozhynska; Fotosmurf03; JBryson; anuwat meereewee.
Back cover: GettyImages: GlobalP; Shootingstar22; Smokeyjo.

Photo Credits:
Dougie-Jason LeBlanc, 48;

PNGTree: kissclipart-3 talk-bubble-png-comic-clipart-speech-balloon-carto, 52-53; beautiful floral frame_5009209 R2A Design, 4, 35; 588ku, 23, 24, 29, 30, 31

Thinkstock Photos: larryrains, 2, 29, 30, 43, 48, 27, 41, 50; seamartini, 52, 53, 40, 41, 40, 53; Moriz89, 13, 36, 56, 13, 38; Vectalex, 13;

Getty Images: Tigatelu, 1, 5, 23, 25, 52, 59; Olga Kurbatova, 18, 20, 46; Vitalii Barida, 3; blueringmedia, 1; hermandesign2015, 4, 17, 21, 47; Rohit Kumar, 63; ChrisGorgio, 43; colematt, 62; William Reagan, 2; McIninch cartoon, 50; IvanMordvinkin, 60; Sonja Filitz, 38; Vitalli Barida, 60; SpicyTruffel, 1; Ian_Redding, 28; Dreamcreation, 59; Henk Bogaard, 53; cofeee, 51; Katya Marchenko, 48, 49; NatuskaDPI, 63; Nataba, 41; Vitalii Barida, 61; AnnaGreen, 11; Svaga, 36; nataka, 1; Bill Ferngren cartoon, 62; M-Reinhardt, 53; HitToon, 5; Mykhailo Ridkous, 14, 16; rvika, 4, 6,8; soleg, 6; Boris_Kuznets, 18; delpixart, 13; mdmilliman, 20; lilu330, 10; yukipon, 52; edb3_16, 4; McIninch, 7; halfpoint, 14; Dushanka, 26; RGTimeline, 9; Geerati, 5; katie ellement, 16; Konstantin Shramchevskiy, 9; Alberto Duran, 12; JimmyLung, 8; Azaliya, 11; tatianazaets, 10, 12; Tammi Mild, 10; hanaschwarz, 5; Vladimir Zapletin, 15; Capuski, 22; Brekbit, 6; PamWalker, 15; mimosa studio, 10, 55; OceanProd, 8; ONYXprj, 17; intst, 22; jentakespictures, 20; Smederevac, 23; Canetti, 24; FooTToo, 16; Jodie777, 19; Prathaan, 24; Onyx Pri, 17; N-sky, 25; nataka, 18; Mykhailo Ridkous 300, 54, 56; TAW4, 58; blueringmedia, 42; kadmy, 29; miskokordic, 27; Roberto, 32; boggy22, 37; Laures, 33; Jupiterimages, 28; Tungalag Balzhirova, 30; Ksenia Raykova, 32; Chonnipa Aranwari, 34; tatyana_tomsickova, 34; Katherine Draxl, 35; unclepodger, 27; Dmytro Beridze, 26; urosr, 26; graphic-bee, 31; musri, 46; denis_pc, 39; GlobalP, 35; Natalia Darmoroz, 48; Nigel Harris, 45; passengerz, 45; WesAbrams, 38; Dmytro Beridze, 32, 34; ASHMISH, 39; bazilfoto, 35; Sonja Filitz, 38; demianvs, 44; graphic-bee, 31; Nicholas Smith cartoon light, 36, 39; Say-Cheese, 45; Cavan Images, 43; krodere, 42; Appfind, 40; paulacobleigh, 41; Rehlik, 42; Andi Edwards, 47; Nils Hasenau, 44; K_Thalhofer, 44; memoangeles, 41; Ksenia Shestakova, 36; volody10, 37;familylifestyle, 50; Lubo Ivanko, 47; Capuski, 48; SuwanPhoto, 46; Bigandt_Photography, 48; Ksuksa, 49; guss95, 46; PamWalker68, 57; Hillebrand Breuker, 52; igorr1, 52, Jpr03, 49; fpphotobank, 50; Gaussian_Blur, 51, A E Cohen, 51; Erick Laubach, 57;Bogdan Kurylo, 19; Urvashi9, 63; Babayev, 57; Nadezhda1906, 54; Milovan Zrnic, 60; bksrus, 62; BlazenImages, 58; Mark Alexander, 56; alex_ugalek, 55; alisa24, 21; dmf87, 54; Mary Miller, 60; fotorince, 59; driftlessstudio, 58; bgsmith, 56; grafvision, 61; flyparade, 61; Halfpoint, 61; Lex20, 63; FotoGablitz, 62; Lightguard, 55;

Produced with the assistance of the Government of Alberta.

Printed in China
PC: 38-1